greasy boot parade

26 poems for alberta, canada

by mike sluchinski

contents

banff bear talker twice

brown blur
(I mean blur fast)
        so soft behind the green opens
        and closes those trees there
        between them then and twice
        and then slow
        enough
brown blur
see the ears there
and a shoulder and
        paws under
        paws over there too
        near the trunks tree trunk
        stumps standing still
for a spell drinks down the
(I mean blur fast)
        down near the puddle potholed
        standing so still
        and no lips
        can't see
        but nose in drinking in
        and then a head
        shake and shake
wet drips shook
(I mean brown blur fast)
and can hear that
did you hear that
        rumble grunt hear that(he' so furry)
        grumble and see him
        see him scratching that
       tree guess so guess we
        really lucked out
never told us

(you look pale)

before we went
just a little hike (you ok)
never said nothing
about bears in banff

(you look pale)
a beautiful day that
and the bear
to think we almost missed

boots aside

photo credit: ©mike sluchinski 2024

drayton valley mustang told me so

down there they
      said it said it sure they did
      down drayton valley
      they got a mustang down at the legion
      up on a pole
      not a horse
      the old plane she is and

and they said you
      sure could do worse
      (the way things are going now boys)
      sure could
      sure you could
      do worse
      than coming out

to drayton valley
      the planes on a pole
      that old mustang still
      (the way things are going now boys)
      got wind
      got wind beneath her wings

still up in the air and i'd agree
agree you sure could
seen a lot of people down there
      the legion and the valley
      sure they got oil
      oil and more

so they say
could do worse
sure could
      and sure nice to see that old plane
      too and have a little

remember
about those that
that served
made a difference like
paid a price
and tell the free riders
(the way things are going now boys)
told them
a thing or two

dancing so blue green (lake louise the color)

out there
lake loiuse and she sounds
    so corny but
  the water the water so
   water (by another name moraine something)
  blue me green me and
  want to dance it down there
  and meet water and lapping tongues and
  frolic if I could

not saying not would
           i like it i'd love
           it got the color up high
           and down low and
           got the color
           sprinkle the pebbles
           and splash and

and huck some rocks out
           there and ripple it
           like the grateful dead and
           einstein two times the money
           and no shade all paid
           playing with waves
           just an emerald pool
           my jade delight
           genie not a bottle
           what three wishes

careful on the rocks
and a slide there
and here and
some splashed up
never stained nothing

except the
memory

lake louise the color

the mall's a mall (free parking)

that's the mall
and like it
(second second biggest big)
or not
the malls a mall
you can walk it or meet some friends
and like to go

            yah sure like to go
            no not tacky
            just a mall and all
            and lotsa stuff
            and a good time too

friends of mine
sure my friends
    like I said friends (not me really)
    yah not a friend story really friends
    had a time down there
    bourbon street even
    good gumbo 'bon temps'
    just like the real thing
    no not joking the mall

long and got halls and mini
golf too or used too at least
leastaways
she's big and she's ours
and that's who we (second second biggest big)
            yah the mall I still like it
            after everything nice so nice
            to walk and talk a
            bit wander like
            have a bite to
            eat and sit and chat

they got a perfume shop too
smells good and nice people
a lot of places with
with maybe
even free parking
if that don't beat it all

boots in hand

photo credit: ©mike sluchinski 2024

edmonton and the other guys for the cup

too cold for football
(won't even say who)
those guys
some kinda team
all east
we're out west
        and for the cup
        to boot
        and a quick
        punt and pass
        back and rally
        down there
        down the field
        run and pass
        and tackle and
        punt and not

interception on
the 40 yard line
not really a ball
just something soaring thrown
pigskin bird get a grip
grip it near the hip nestle some
wrestle and pass

until whistles and halftime and
so cold with no
rest snow something
snow coming tonight

and if the 'o' line doesn't and
the 'd' line doesn't get you
a quick one touchdown pass

and a punt

MIKE SLUCHINSKI

popped up

the weather probably will
(wonder if they brought their woolies)

deern dodge outside oyen deern headlights

deer party gone
wrong
     crashed through
         the conway twitty night
     due west (crow flies) but at night
     way the worst part way worse
     moving to
     calgary going back
with a load
and hope drifts
black night ice bright
and two deer
killed the truck

no grill left
and the one who
missed the dodge
wound up in the ditch
run off

devil heart hillside legs joust
     hit and sit and run
     haunches high hop
     antlers and a hop
skip jump
and the hills
     near oyen just outside the limits
     and couldn't find
     drove in and the RCMP not
     answering the pick up
        phone just a number
     no lights and a 97
        totalled off dodge

my scrap now sold so high and a punch
gut punch and leftover fur on the trim
waiting in the wings angels nearby
that and bent steel hissing rad
and a two good shuteyes
still in session
lamplight bright

boots in sight

photo credit: ©mike sluchinski 2024

buffalo in flight

out past hanna closer
to delia they run
herd of bison by
another name
buffalo
            and they're
            devils in fur
            coats no matter
            how you cut it the best last hope

and like to see them run
            stop and see them
            run there and back
            every time before
            the turn to drumheller

like to see them run
they turn this way
            and that
            fly east west across the fields
            and autograph the pasture with it
          hoofs and hoof pounded rounded too
            through the wires they look and stare
            there they go
            flutter like birds and they watch
            always a lookout
            those black eyes
            no wonder in them no wander

they're good eating
and i want a
            a skull for the wall
            train a crow to pick
            it clean or maybe

a coyote
(if he don't run off with it)
but don't tell the wife
she likes them too

big tipi change

there's power to change
and pow
wow change and
old ernie never
       asked for much
       of either
       and neither would
       anyone really not
       after the dust and streets
       and what little rain
       pass the hat

fifty winters downtown
medicine hat and
all that they got a college
now and there's pow wows in season

american cousins and a visit
sometimes hunting
if someone takes
            him out
            he got a turkey feather
            for his hat decent
            boots heels just a little
            worn in step side step they
            shook his hand some
            city guy did mayor maybe

next day down
on the corner old ernie
could see him
looking for spare change

hand up
hand out

so short changed

nine lives may

wop whatta name
shoulda had nine lives
        cat man
        none better nicknames
        don't say it all
all aces he was
walked away
        crashes and all
        said it was dumb luck the
        baron didn't get
        him (that kinda guy)

nearly died a dozen
times cats woulda run out woulda
run out of them (lives)
this was an albertan
nobody made him one
        just was
        just rightly was
        just a hero let alone

story couldn't make it
up one pirate eye
movies tried songs too
        and sung the stories
        didn't know when to
        stop and so

if they ask you about alberta
tell them about the guy
who fell from the sky only
        had one good eye
        and as long as there's alberta
wop may

the story
never die

this was an albertan
and then some

boots we glow

photo credit: ©mike sluchinski 2024

lost the benz in calgary

driving around there
around the mall just
(not the parking place)
south and there's
an overpass
(covers some kind of big road)
and exit
(some kind of turnaround place)

but before that set of lights set
up no snow or ice just a good
road and our old benz our
sturdy girly

so stopping should
have been should
so easy and by the time
stopped for the red that
little truck behind
us a ways didn't couldn't
wouldn't and hit us
right

rear ended up like an old
timey crumpled crumple
means hit so hard
she did and had no trunk left
some kind hatched back
hunch back almost
my lunch back

some kind of bobby
vinton accordion
hit totaled off too
accordion my eye

castor road kill (cold shoulders and damp ditches)

woke up up
woke us right up and
        outside castor
        somewhere just
        out of castor and
        a turn and it wasn't
        that late not late but
        he never saw us

truck way too
over and out my lane
so close he could kiss me
and never thought a crown vic
would ever be too small to well
notice

but he never saw us
and must have just
woke up pulled into our lane and
        steering hard
        white knuckles and all
        and cursing too you
        know how you know
        who and almost

hit the ditch
off the shoulder
whistling weeds
and he don't quit
        just right on
        going not knowing
        (nothing over easy about it)
        but got his plates

followed him

only one road
and made the call
those rcmp call center
some truck just almost
almost hit the ditch
with me in it

nisku highway overnights

storms for stopping
midnight waltz over to
blackjacks and a rumble down
truck stop parking spot rigside
ringside ringers and all night service
a nice safe lot

white line picket fences
windows show furry pair a dice
and green county mounties
on dark nights for a good price
no free camping clean scrubbed
restrooms coffee laundry hot
hot coffee all night long

play it again pony up
happy faces and a good place
parking after hours rain and
roadwork black top
smiling bright wheel row
grins promise late nights
early morning rumble diesel
smoke and harvest dust
bacon breakfast
over easy mornings

few hours for hours shuteye
red eye and pimento olive pits
the pits parking palace nisku
mansion highway side just
at nisku can't don't wanna
miss it sleepin the back
centerfolds half peeled
cowboy boots cowboy roots

steal a line and cheap cheroots
wine tipped kickers and
bassett hounds
called claude
rhymes with load
(yes there was a dog in the cab)

mundare sausage pick up trucks and real smoke

16 highway runs so so
straightly round small
small lakes and a hill
hill or two maybe
going to mundare

and another easter run
past the holiday passed
reasons for mundare
are over there for
sausage and a third
generation run of the mill
or hill and stop for sausage

and their fine grind smoked garlic
and more from people with names
like mine no one can say
except (how do you spell that)
ukrainian what

can't say i have said someone
run down and kept moving
past down and down that road and
rail it was a long ago trail and a paint to ride it
(didn't even get horses til the 20s)

and a lot of how do you spell that like
stopped off into the new life
you know the kind

good sausage and mundare
again smoked ham and a turnaround
easter again
with the unpronounceables
(how do you spell that)

ukrainian what

good sausage i said
love the name
just the same
just like mine
good sausage
everytime

fort mac and the fire giant

never was the same
like they said after
watched it on
the teevee

and the lines of cars but
not really mostly trucks
and black ones at that
and they headed out
all of them just going
(what could they)

and the after
the after
after it was
all said all done
just ash ash ash
gray rain it all again

and burnt out places up there
(block by block)
block by block in places
and nothing to come to
to come back to to
come back for the news
bad teevee worse and all
lines leaving
ant farms to the horizon

they going to come back
ever or not
nobody got a crystal
ball not much really
left of it all

smoking in to canmore

not many done it
    like that and not
    many would want
    to in a tow truck no less

with a kia loaded
        up on the
        back and another
        hyundai in the drag
        behind rock a bye
        cradle wheels
        (they hook on kind)
        (piggy back but not really)

and we were hauled
(like the cars)
driver didn't see
talking to much
one of the tires on the cradle
rock a bye bye
        blew and rubber everywhere
        and kept on keeping going
        until the rim hit the road
        no rubber to speak of
        sparks flew we weren't
        in love sparks flew
        like an angle grinder to a metal road
        sparks flew (and smoke too)

but the tow truck guy kept
yip yip yippin until
        o jeez we blew a tire
        (more smoke more sparks)
        kept it rolling

a few more miles
kind of didn't look safe
even with the ambers on

at the dealer drop
canmore they changed the tire
never seen the likes
and some choice words too
before nor since

highway to calgary (see those lights over there)

down highways seven and nine
west headed and then some
huckle buckle highway my way
and then come they came
went whatever way and most
coming with you with

guessed it
not much at all
a suitcase and a
we'll buy some furniture with
the first paycheck and so they went and
still they come calgary bound

government town too red
deer and the rest for work
and a better job and
new starts and hey my cousins there
or uncle or business
alberta becoming

oil in the blood breathing gas or a
good school grad school
              some found money just add water
              some found fame and name
              some found happy i guess
              some found nothing
              at all except they
              never had to go back
              where they came from
              but never really were from

dumps you know and just
can't love so board it up tear
it down kind of there

MIKE SLUCHINSKI

those dead little one streets

the sunset sets
the west and rises too
and i'll see you too
see you soon
out calgary
(see those lights over there)

boots in double

photo credit: ©mike sluchinski 2024

passing canmore on the way (for blair richardson)

not much like the
sun out in canmore and on any
any day seems summer winter
eternal sky sight bulging break out

both ways coming and going there's
good horsey sun and tremble
light both ways looks like mountains

high like an old style
viewmaster just click
clicking through push the button
down and not the dragon face
and more and gray rocky breath
gravel days and crunch underfoot
and hiking boots grin and peck

sometimes evening black
sometimes morning blue and the
clouds just clouds bounce float by up
you could pop them with a pin
there and the black slate grate

so pass me by all the way
passing through canmore too
coming out

both ways coming and going there's
good horsey sun and tremble
light both ways looks like mountains

riverside off road by hinton

get out of the car and
stretch a stretch after
hours sitting the
back stretch
just off the
highway

just the river
running fast ripples running by
shaking sheets outside the line
rock sandwich and salads
and round and
a low bank easy to get
down and soak a little there

muddy too mulberry wash
so go down and water
waters blue green
like jade polished
green smiles mirror back

and socks come off
bent and toes hug the
step rocks step by and all
and bent knees one toe out front

crabbing careful and just shaken
step for a quick and quiet dip
pitter patter grip
and toes sink ankle deep skin too
glacier ice pack six pack
ahhhhhhh ahhhhhhh and
breathe so deep
dared to
you would too

peace river maybe chinese food

don't keep asking
and again again
repeating now and
look for one already
if that's what you want
        it's a long ways yet
        it's hours hours away hours
        up to you up to you
        up there and
        who knows what
        the foods like out there

don't know so look
look it up you got time
you want to drive
you said you
wanted some so
        okay call them just
        call already ask
        them ask at the
        next stop gas
        station phone already
        someone knows

must be in town
call already sure
maybe mebbe mebbe
just ask them
they speak English
        i'm good with
        it sure love it
        love it greasy maybe it will be
        never been so call already extra
        plum and soy don't forget

fortune cookies and an
eggroll just don't get any
on the leather

cops calgary crowchild

get places easy on crowchild
on the trail but
           better be
           careful on
           crowchild

and not too fast
too fast you know
you want to go
faster but
           they're there with
           (you know parked on the side)
           with those trick
           speed doohickeys
           and vroom vroom
           just blazes fast black
           little trucks they are fast
         and still have cherries
           on them (see them too
           too late even red ones)

those calgary cops you
           know be easy you be
           be terrible careful
           because it's easy
           so easy the way she
           she goes with
           just a tap and
           pedal pusher you know it

after one forty
yes the one four oh
well you know
they just

(justmight)
take your
car

boots high step

photo credit: ©mike sluchinski 2024

beef dip calgary you know who (au jus they call it)

that's the
>
> problem the problem
> it's cooked so slow
> melt almost or near to it
> so slow the
> slow cooking and
> the sauce that's where

where it's tricky
>
> too with the thin sliced
> slices and some like
> it different no way
> to say no way to
> to count for taste
> account for it

up to you
>
> and better be
> and there's no
> one way to or the
> highway some
> cheese or not some say not

or both ways or not
it's the thin
thin sliced beef
>
> good beef not
> dirty old stringy stuff
> not just cow
> you better believe
> it and horseradish some fight for
> brown mustard smoky
> stuff some want yellow
> and french too but

but a fresh roll or
nothing and
then the
dip
   au jus
   they call it
open up
just say alberta beef

edmonton for extra pickles

there's food for
food for thought
                and then there's just
                you know the
                eating kind and
                i'll tell you

not shy neither
not shy about it
drove for
it and that much
that much for certain

I don't know
                don't know about
                the changes
                we changed a bunch a
                lot (alberta did)
                alberta changed the
                the city too
                a lot of new

new people and all
some say good
        and i got mine
          and some they
          just don't care
          but i'll tell you (not shy neither)
          i got in the (not shy about it)
          the truck and drove
          down to edmonton

down there
off the highway
just for that (not shy neither)

MIKE SLUCHINSKI

shwarma (not shy about it)
extra pickles
please careful
with that hot sauce

wetaskiwin train bends tracks too

don't know for
>> how many miles
>> before the tracks
shift or
turn or what
>> they just keep on
>> keep on and then a train
you can see it
can't you
>> then a train come
>> by and rumble on
these days like
painted circus cars
>> some in the yards
>> painted them up like
elephant trains and wrote
crazy all over the place
>> and paint too
>> you know it
not just here
you know it all kinds of
>> colors
>> some of them nice
i saw some near
the city they were
>> but they roll by to just the
>> rails stay put
and hold tight
all like they were
>> a married couple
>> holding on and down
all pinned down
ties and spikes

pinned to the maps
but not paper to the earth
and grass
just like steel
roads
and folds

weld you a new one

they come out in a black one
the truck that is and drove up and
went to work straight to
work right to it and lit up the
torches and all fire breathing

mask and all smoke too there was
work enough and torches were hot
and running and a long day too
and not much more to say so

brought out coffee like you should
they earned it all that and after all
time for a break but there was
noise and all and the bunch of them

just working away
so I fired a warning shot (the sights are gone)
said coffees on into the air
(me with the rifle)

and called coffees on
and i saw them drop down some
rolling lost their hat
and another mask off tugging
rubbing themselves on the
down the ground

the foreman looked up he
did he looked me straight
and said straight in the eye it was

lady

you do that again you do that again
and I'll weld you a new one

so I said and I said you look here
(me with the rifle)
look here

you so and so (me with the rifle)
you scared of an old lady

boots in waiting

photo credit: ©mike sluchinski 2024

out in banff never went

out in banff
had the wedding
the wedding out there
(she's a castle some say)
so they did

and sure was invited got the invite and all
and they did they did ask
just never went and
can't remember why
the place you know

the big place
there the big one
hotel yah hotel and all
(she's a castle some say)
went there a couple times but never
made the wedding and

and it sure was something
so I heard and
no it's a bit of a price
sure not cheap and
expected more maybe they
changed the old carpets by now
(she's a castle some say)
and sure hope so but

when you go to banff
when you go not sure
not many care
no not many care
about the rugs and all
they might be out
just outside

she's a nice place
more than trees and mountains
 hot springs too bears and squirrels
maybe more to some
maybe less
(she's a castle some say)

ninety something supermarket in edmonton

had them a while back
yah not here not here
but those big broad noodles
what you call them

whatchamacallem come in rolls but
they're noodles sure noodle rolled up
well do you got them
you have them here
whaddya mean maybe maybe not
yes or no my friend

the guys at the restaurant said come
come here something something
ninety something supermarket the big one
yah here downtown chinatown

yah so i'm here got here
well to buy them yah
to buy them if you
got them you gotta cook them
but slice them first

yah they come in rolls
rolled up look at this paper here
rolled up—r-o-ll-e-d-u-p you hear me
ok ok I'll wait

those the ones
sure is sure are and nice ones too
you got more gimme three packs
what are they called
how do i say that how do I say that

ok no idea what you said
as long as you have them

I can come back or what
next time the same ok
you will really you will
or maybe sure I'll come back
ninety something or other

you guys are great
for the noodles

boots next to

photo credit: ©mike sluchinski 2024

19264802R00039